# August 2023

## Miah's Monthly Poetry

## S. H. Miah

Muslim Fiction Project

# CONTENTS

# THIRD COLLECTION

It's the third collection.

I should probably mention

That I intend these collections

To be a lifelong endeavour.

Well, if each one runs

About fifty to a hundred,

Then that's thousands and

Thousands of poems.

That's a little daunting,

Don't you think?

Well, no time like the present

To press paper against ink.

# REDEMPTION

We seek redemption from our past acts,

Our past sins. We seek redemption

From the troubles we have caused

Over all our years. We seek redemption

From the problems we created and then

Never helped to solve. We seek redemption,

But truly, why are we seeking it?


If we redeem ourselves only for ourselves,

Is it truly redemption?

# CONVICTION

Do we lack conviction in the words of Allah?

Many times, a problem arises, and the first

Port of call is not The Qur'an. Instead we

Rush to Tom, Dick, and Harry. We don't realise

That the creation can only help us so far.

In the end, all help extends back to Allah.

# SITTING WITH A FRIEND

I'm sitting with a friend

Before a park, and around the bend

Of the iron gate lies

Flowers, pink, yellow, and red,

An assortment of colours,

No mere trend, but the beauty

Of nature with its wings spread.

A scene I don't wish to forget.

# Colours

Everyone experiences colours differently.

A spectrum of red, blue, and green.

Yet we all filter those three

Through our eyes when we see.

And we see different shades,

Your turquoise might be my navy,

My red might be your purple or pink,

Your green might not be my cup of gravy.


So why be racist

If my black or white

Or every shade in between

Could be the exact opposite

To what you see?

# OBLIGATION

Salah is an obligation,

But it shouldn't feel like one.

Sometimes, the walk to the mosque

Feels like *hijrah* from one street to the next,

A journey of months and years,

Across seas and continents.

Shaytan's whispers are, indeed, always near.

# Rush

Don't rush when embarking on something new.

Don't you want the initial excitement to last you

From trough to trough? Or will it wear off

Before you can even reach the peak built for you?

# WORDS

Words have meaning, have power,

Have rhyme schemes built like a tower,

Each brick placed with a succinctness,

Carefully laid out like the petals of a flower.

But sometimes,

The words rush,

Gush forth like a

Never ending stream,

Lush like the water

Lapping at the sea,

As the tide rolls in.

Or maybe it's a tornado

Of thoughts,

Rumbling and tumbling,

Whirling and swirling,

Syllables hurling themselves

To the end of the poem.

# Toxic

How many times in our life

Do we ingest the toxins,

Hoping the other person dies?

# CYCLES

We are all on journeys,

Up and down the lows and highs,

Round the cycle till the day we die.

So why do we glance

At the peaks of others,

Yet stare at the

Troughs of our life?

# Whispers

I see an imposition,

An exposition,

From the devil every time

He calls me to his expeditions.


Follow footsteps, yeah I'd do it,

And then what? Admonition,

From Allah, The Most High,

About the consequences.


We cannot escape the punishment,

That will befall us if we don't even comprehend,

Returning back to him, hands up in repentance,

And trying our level best to fight those satanic whispers.

# NEEDS

Without food or drink,

Our bodies will break down.

Without breathing oxygen,

Our lungs would collapse.

Without *dhikr* of Allah,

Will our souls cope with *dunya's* attacks?

# PURPOSE

The purpose of an object is given by the maker,

Or the owner, or the sustainer.

Allah does all three,

For us, His creation,

And yet we attempt to find our

Purpose outside the one He's given?

# Sweetness

I have never

Witnessed someone leave Islam,

Having already

Tasted the sweetness of Iman.

Taste it,

Let the sweetness fill you up.

Then you'll

Find yourself avoiding the haram.

# WRIST PAIN

I suffered with wrist pain

From typing too much.

Pinky was getting strained

On the right side,

Like a right winger

Running up the sides

All match long,

Hammies on their last legs.

I had to switch to the home row,

And the typing flow slowed,

And my fingers felt cold,

Speed now a crawl,

Making baby steps as the muscle

Memory struggled to catch on

To my intentions, brain and body

Almost severed, with weak connections.

But *Alhamdulillah*, new changes

Begin slow, but end up better

Than whatever we had before.

# THE GYM

Oddly,

The gym

Characterises life in

A way that's so

Ghastly accurate.

Think on it,

Friend.

# Pyramid Scheme

Success is merely a series of small steps.

But we all want it fast, want it to be next

In our achievements, like it's on a bucket list.

And what's next? Happiness, with a fast car,

Lamborghini Aventador, and a huge house,

An expensive seven bedroom masterclass.

And what else? What other illusions of this *dunya*

Can your mind think about? Is that truly the success

We should be seeking out? Or are we being duped,

Like loving this dunya is Shaytan's pyramid scheme,

So he can drag everyone into the fiery pits of hell?

# QUESTIONS

Can you imagine gaining everything—

Money, wealth, the biggest house,

Cars that can spin round and round

For hours and hours,

But you can never speak to another living soul?

Would you accept it?

Or is it those around us that make life life,

As opposed to the material world

Towards which we strive?

# MATERIAL

Look into yourself,

And into the hearts of others,

For indeed more gems lie there

Than in the material outside.

These bodies are only temporary,

But our souls, on the inside,

Will eventually last forever,

But the destination Allah will decide.

# LOTTERY

Society is like the lottery.

Everyone wishes to win,

But at the expense of who?

Each other. Whilst the Shaytans

At the top are the true winners,

Stirring the pot of crabs

Who are trying to steal from each other.

# Overtake

Not everyone has your back.

Some wish to attack

The very things which you lack,

As if they are perfect beings.


What we should be seeing

Are the faults within our being,

Faults which are anything but fleeting,

Faults which we can change.


But is our changing range

Able to fan the flames

Of our sins, minor and grave,

Or will we let them overtake?

# HOME RUNS

Pat yourself on the back,

Rise when you fall on the mat.

Because you are your biggest fan,

And you're the only one to wield the bat

And score home runs, just like that.

# LANGUAGE

Isn't it amazing?

Language is just a bunch of scribbles,

Like dribbles of ink, splodging paper

Into which it then sinks.

And yet, from these little squiggles,

Little black marks,

We can form a lifetime of stories.

# STANDING OVATION

A standing ovation

Is when everyone stands

To clap for a woman or man's achievement.


But there's another day,

In which we'll all stand,

But who are the ones with the ovation?

# ACHIEVEMENTS

Achievements don't feel good

When you don't work hard.

Yet we live in a culture

Of results coming fast,

As if Jannah will be

Thrust into our palms,

With no reckoning,

No day of judgement.

Choose achievements to strive for,

And in their glows will you bask.

# CARS AND TREES

I look out the window of the bus,

See a car heading by,

With a tree in its above.

The car is perfectly symmetrical,

Innards all electrical,

Running on fumes and petrol,

Yet the tree,

Despite being ancient,

Holds more beauty,

Without the symmetry

Or the electricity.

# FREE

I remember a quote

About man being free

Yet everywhere in chains.

But *everywhere* does not

Include locations outside this *dunya*.

So, indeed, it is the afterlife

In which we will find our freedom.

# CROWDING OUT

The crowding out effect,

In the world of economics,

Is when increases in state spending,

Lowers that of the private sector.


Are we like this,

Wherein we enter a group of friends,

And crowd them all out,

Instead of bringing out their gifts?

# GIFTS

We have been given, by Allah,

Gifts which we cannot enumerate.

Exuberant bodies, fresh air,

Food of which the kings of old would dream.

It is wholly unbelievable,

That after all these gifts,

Someone would disbelieve,

Or worse yet mock and deceive.

Be thankful for your gifts,

And they shall, indeed, increase.

# REMEMBERING HIM

Every day,

She sits on the bench,

Remembering him.


He had curly long hair,

Waving down to his ears,

An easy smile

That turned her frown upside down.


He was strong, resolute,

Could tear a chimney from its chute,

Cut logs out in the woods,

Could slaughter a cow for its food.

His heart was laid open,

Like a book that was spoken

Into her heart that was broken,

When his life had finally frozen.


Every day,

She sits on the bench,

Remembering him.


And she remembers that,

In the afterlife,

They will finally be reunited.

# Balance

Too little laundry wastes the pods.

Too much can turn your clothes to sods.

What we need is the middle balance,

The perfect amount.

In most things, timing is everything,

Rather than a count.

# WORRYING

What's the point of worrying,

If it only increases worrying?

Action is what takes our mind

Away from the intrusive thoughts.

Action cannot be bought,

It's a habit that cannot be taught.

But action is what causes

All your worries to melt from your core.

# FIRDAWS AL-A'LA

How is it that we will marvel

At a millionaire's car,

Or their watch,

Or their yacht?

Yet they'd trade everything they have,

For a sip of Jannah's waters,

Which are promised to us,

If we shake off this dunya,

And work for the hereafter.

So wrap your belts tighter.

Against Shaytan become a fighter.

Aim higher and higher.

So you can reach *firdaws al-a'la*.

# PLAN

Sometimes,

We look back,

Into our past.

The successes.

The failures.

And we slowly realise

That there was a plan,

A plan from Allah,

That everything

We thought

That was either

Good or bad,

Has a purpose

For us now.

And that realisation

Makes us glad.

# NOSTALGIA

He feels a hit of nostalgia.

It grips his heart, like the squeeze

Of his late mother's embrace.

The smells are even the same,


Lavender with a hint of iris.

He breathes it in, steps inside the gate.

He recalls the summers of play,

Surrounded by long gone mates.


The grass shimmers in the sun,

Radiant with a glow never undone,

As if that image from his childhood

Has from his past become unstuck.


But the entire place will be run amok,

With construction workers, contractors,

Turning the place to rubble, and building

On it their industrial building projects.


He projects that in ten years' time,

Every sight of his past will be demolished

To make way for houses, for other things.

And the thought really does sadden him.

# DREAMS

Sometimes,

I read writers years ahead of me,

In skill and in experience,

And I doubt I'll ever be

Able to ride their coattails,

Able to smell the dust they leave behind.

But I pray Allah allows me to surpass them,

If only because the Ummah needs

Writers who are skilled, experienced,

And can cause Muslims to motivate.

# TRANSCENDENCE

I love my mother.

And I'm glad to be a Muslim.

It means there will be a time

In which that fear

Of her passing away

Will no longer be in existence.

# Molecule

Our existence here

Is merely a drop in an ocean,

Or even less, a single molecule.

Microscopic, utterly ineffectual.

And yet we chase this molecule,

Instead of the ocean which follows it.

# April 11th, 2013

That was the last time she saw him.

Her husband, her rock in life,

Had been lying in that white bed,

Under those white covers,

Innocent like a dove's flight,

Soaring high above the world,

As if already in heaven.

She remembers how, not a day before,

She'd laughed with him, and smiled,

And thought he would never be gone.

But April 11th came,

Over a decade ago,

And she still feels the pain.

A pain that may never let go.

# WITH GUILT

If you must sin,

Then sin with guilt

That tears your heart to pieces.

Because, indeed in that guilt

Lies faith that can

Transform sinful turmoil

Into an eternal peace.

# THE HEART

The heart is a fickle thing.

It yearns what is not

Good for its body,

Yet hates what

Can save itself.

It is as if the heart

Cannot tell

That it is causing

Its own destruction.

# LIKE DUST

Sins are like dust.

Sometimes invisible,

And seemingly insignificant.

But the deviance of sins

Come in the shape of sickness,

Just like the dust can

Be a silent infector.

And it is a reality we all witness.

# STILTS

Sometimes,

Life feels like a struggle,

Feels like it's rubble

As opposed to the castle,

We all dreamed of.


But castles can be rebuilt,

And so can our lives,

Even if for some time,

We move around on stilts.

# BUILT

Rome wasn't built in a day.

So why do we try to rebuild

Ourselves in that time frame?

After all, aren't we striving

For much greater than Rome?

A place called Jannah,

A place we wish to call home.

# PROTECTION

He comes home looking drunk out his mind.

Hits the counter, his head looking like a bee hive.

Smells of piss, of vodka mixed with rotten chives.

Tastes like his stomach acid has been fried.


He opens his palm, sees the scratches within.

Knows that he caused them, digging his nails in.

He's lost so much blood that every drop feels a win.

He reaches for the bottle again with a grin.


But deep within he knows he's in the wrong.

The realisation hits his heart like a gong.

His resolve feels weaker than his grip feels strong.

But the bottle slips, glass shattering like a song.


"Dammnit," he says, wooziness coming on.

He swirls on his feet, drunkenness like a con.

*Come on,* he thinks, stares at the spilt alcohol.

And he breathes in deep, hates himself even more.


The booze wears off over the next few hours,

And still he stares at the spilt drink with a glower.

But he knows it's a blessing that the drink has soured.

It's a protection, since in the end it's him the sin devours.

# Sinkholes

Sins create sinkholes.

The greater the sins,

The bigger the hole.

And all it takes is one slip

For someone to fall

All the way to Jahannam.

# DELAY

If Allah immediately brought down the punishment,

For our disobeying His commandments,

Or our falling into His prohibitions,

Then we would all be dead,

An infinite times over, for our sins.

The fact Allah delays our punishment

Is a blessing of time for repentance.

# STRANGE

Isn't it strange that those who say

Allah does not exist

Are constantly plagued with thoughts about Him?

How strange that one can ponder God,

If one does not believe

The concept, in the first place, exists?

# BOIL

Let your anger be

More like water,

And less like milk.

Because milk boils over,

Whilst water boils under.

# BREAKFAST

Breakfast is the most important meal,

But not because it's the food we need.

I think it's because of the routine,

Which jump-starts our early mornings,

So we can be productive as much as needed.

# TIMES

Mornings are the most blessed times.

Sometimes, my productivity shoots to the sky,

And each word written feels like a high,

And the poetry and prose feels sublime.

But what I have to realise

Is that success is not defined

By the height of the good times,

But by how high we can keep the bad times.

# MODERATION

Water is the tastiest thing

When we are parched beyond belief.

But after a time it becomes sickening.

With everything, even water, moderation is key.

So don't become that person who eats

The world's treasures till he pukes and bleeds.

Because, indeed, that person never succeeds.

# ARTIFICIAL

I can have as much junk food as I want.

But strangely, rather paradoxically,

The hearty homemade meals

Are the ones that satisfy me the most.

It is as if the artificial

Can have no bearing on the natural,

Despite how hard we work

To make it seem so.

# OLD RELATIONSHIP

He remembers young Stacy.

His old haram relationship.

He remembers the feelings

Which he had back then.


There was the excitement

Of doing something forbidden.

There was the temptation

Of falling into deeper sin.


There was the worry

Of his father finding out.

There was the dread

Of knowing it wouldn't work out.


There were the endless nights

Of texting till *fajr*.

There were the sleepless days,

Of trying to make things work.


He remembers breaking up,

The angst and the hurt,

The subsequent temper tantrums,

Like a dam had been burst.


But now he has a wife—

Much better than young Stacy—

With whom he can grow old.

He wouldn't trade her for the world.

# OVER TIME

Over time, we can achieve

The wildest of our dreams,

The deepest of our wants,

The highest of our peaks.


But we all seek these things too fast and

The first two words are the most important.

# OVERTIME

Islam is not a 9 to 5.

You can't just work it full time.

You have to spend that overtime

Over a long period of time.

Then the rewards,

Like regular overtime,

Are far greater.

# FIVE PILLARS

There's a swivel chair before me.

Sleek, black all round,

High back so the shoulders don't slouch.

The chair reminds me of Islam,

Because there are five legs

Holding it in place, holding it together,

Like our religion's core five pillars.

# CAFFEINE

I always had a problem with coffee.

Used to drink three a day,

As if it kept the doctor away.

I would even go as far as to say

That I drank the beverage religiously.

Then I went on a coffee vacay,

Decided to switch it out for a change,

Didn't drink it for months and days,

And then decided to have a sip again.

And by God did the palpitations palpitate,

And now I avoid all caffeine like the plague.

# SLEEP

Too much sleep sometimes

Feels worse than too little.

My eyes get bleary,

Heavy like an iron fiddle.

My legs feel like lead

That I sledge across the middle

Of my bedroom, in an attempt

To get downstairs. Then a single

Step at the bottom makes me tumble

To the ground. And the pain sizzles

Like turkey bacon on a grill.

And I regret sleeping in,

Because the extra sleep has

Somehow made my life a riddle.

# OUTLINES

I don't outline before I write.

So writing fiction

Feels like reading the

Story for the first time.

Exhilarating, enthralling, sublime.

I don't make up the story.

It's more like the story makes me.

# Morals

When the teacher says

Not to rock on the chair,

There's always a story

Attached to the fare.

"He fell back on his head

And his blood was a mess."

We all know they're lying.

"That never happened," we said.

But the teachers know

What we all know.

That stories are the thread

That infuses morals into our head.


Allah doesn't just tell us morals.

Sometimes, He uses stories

To convey them. Indeed,

Those true stories are the best.

# KNOTS

We spend so much time

Untangling a knot.

When what we need is to

Step back, look along the line,

Take in the bigger picture,

And realise that knot is only

A bump in the grand

Scheme of our lives.

# BRITISH WEATHER

British summer time,

Glorious in our lives.

Sunny with a venomous shine,

Raining in picturesque lines.

Not storms or tornadoes,

But more swings than forest vines.

Honestly, it's like a sordid love affair,

Filled with more than a strange surprise.

# DEBILITATION

Good health only becomes

A priority during bad health.

But is it wise to let in bad times?

Can we not appreciate

Our blessings without needing

To experience debilitation?

# CAPITAL

Experiences are what drive us

To learn, to feel, to love.

So why are we stuck inside,

Whether at home or

In our own heads?

Experience life,

And watch your capital rise.

# O MUSLIM

O Muslim.

You are

Not weak,

Not dishevelled,

Not meek,

Not mellowed,

Not in deceit,

Not just another fellow.

You are a worshipper of Allah,

The Most High, The Magnificent.

And that, truly, is special.

# A Word

Remember your *duas*,

Even when absent minded.

That single word

Could be the difference,

Between your heaven

And hellfire.

# SMILE

When was the last time

You saw someone's face,

And a smile immediately graced yours?

Hold onto those people,

Because they have a trait,

Of the Prophet (SAW) of The Lord.

# Poison

Sometimes we view everyone as toxic,

In every environment we enter.

But even a drop of poison

Can sully the water,

And we have to question:

Are we that drop of toxin?

# SECRET INGREDIENT

I love all kinds of curry.

Lamb meat with its savoury taste,

Chicken so succulent, never to waste.

Maybe *korma*, with its warm, soothing paste.

What about fish curries? I cannot complain.

And don't get me started on the plethora

Of choices, when it comes to veggie curries,

It feels like I've been spoiled.

Spinach with the jackfruit seeds,

Sitting in my stomach after I feed.

But what I adore the most about any curry,

Is a secret ingredient

No one can replicate.

Alone it's enough.


That secret ingredient

Is my mother's love.

# Newsletter

For writing updates and info on new releases, sign up to our newsletter!

# About MFP

The Muslim Fiction Project, MFP, is an initiative started by S. H. Miah to publish works of fiction that promote Islamic messages for Muslims all around the world.

Written for Muslims. By a Muslim.

Visit our website to see what other stories you could sink your teeth into!

# About S. H. Miah

S. H. Miah is the founder of Muslim Fiction Project. An initiative to produce high-quality Muslim fiction. Written for Muslims. By a Muslim.

When not writing, S. H. Miah enjoys spending time with family and friends, charging through his own reading list, and of course having a bit too large an obsession with spiral-bound notebooks.

For more information about Muslim Fiction Project, please visit: https://www.muslimfictionproject.com

Milton Keynes UK
Ingram Content Group UK Ltd.
UKHW020730030823
426269UK00014B/517

9 798223 587484